Of Course, I'm a Feminist!

Of Course, I'm a Feminist!

Edited by Ellen Goldberg

A Publication of The Poetry Box®

Library of Congress Control Number: 2015942928

ISBN-13: 978-0986330452
ISBN-10: 0986330450

Published by The Poetry Box®, 2015
Beaverton, Oregon
www.ThePoetryBox.com
530.409.0721

Dedicated to the women
who have bravely lifted their voices,
who have paved the path
toward freedom and equality
and who continue to fight the good fight

Contents

Introduction

When my friend and fellow-poet, Judith Barrington, asked if I'd organize a reading of feminist poetry, I was intrigued – why now? Do some poets still identify that way? What qualifies as a feminist poem? I was, in the Seventies, one of a mass movement of women whose lives were set on fire by women's poetry, whose poetry was changed by seeing the world through new eyes. But if we were going to read feminist poetry in 2015, I didn't want the poems to be a weak echo of those powerfully urgent, but out-of-date, voices. I wanted a reading, grounded in the present, which would inspire an audience to once again unite to be a transformative power.

With this vision in mind, the poems in *Of Course, I'm a Feminist!* were selected for a reading given on March 8, 2015 – International Women's Day – in Portland, Oregon. Forty women had submitted entries. Judging anonymously, I chose one poem each from eighteen different poets. Soapstone, a non-profit organization for the support of women writers, suggested and funded the reading.

I am of the mind that the earthquake of the Civil Rights Movement set into motion a tsunami wave of liberation movements – the anti-Viet Nam War movement, the Women's Movement, the Gay Liberation Movement. The liberation of one group wakes up the longing for freedom in others. This year the rising up against police brutality that started in Ferguson, Missouri reminded the world of how much is yet to be done. Maybe the courage that African Americans are demonstrating across the country against the killing of innocent young black men has the power to set off new waves of liberation – for women to address the still unmet agenda against domestic violence and rape, for childcare, equal pay and an end to crimes against women worldwide.

In the late sixties and early seventies in consciousness-raising groups, women learned to get comfortable speaking our truths out loud to each other. These were intimate truths that came out of our up-until-then, well-hidden private lives. Honor Moore wrote in the anthology, *Poems from the Women's Movement*: "In the process of speaking what was hidden, we began to identify with one another as women to become a *we*." We saw the common threads of our oppression. We were being freed from the delusion that we are separate from each other.

Poetry was remarkably central to the Second Wave of feminism. Honor Moore: "The women's movement *was* poetry." When our truths met up with poetry, they became the North Star by which the Women's Movement set its compass. Poet Audre Lorde urged us on, "Poetry is not a luxury. Poetry is a vital necessity of our existence." Fighting for change has always been made less daunting by our poetry, music, art and dance, the hopeful heartbeats of liberation movements. Especially read aloud, poetry was the ideal vehicle for women to express rage, analysis, grief and humor.

This reading celebrated our foremother poets, and adhered to our values as feminists: we read as a group, no one poet the headliner. Second Wave poems were not obscure or academic. The poems in this volume, like those earlier poems, ring out in the body-centered, emotional, earthy voices of mothers, daughters, survivors and workers.

Women poets in 2015 have not run out of issues to address. These poems take up the cause of our mother's constricted lives. They remind us that women continue to be brutalized by domestic violence and rape. One third of all U.S. single mothers live in poverty today. Millions of women in the world weren't touched by the Second Wave. But our seriousness is tempered by our giving names to our breasts, playing in the mud and calling out to love and imagination, as you'll read in these poems.

One of the poems was written and read by a fifteen year old high school student who makes it clear that she alone can define herself, one by a seventy-three year old farmer and artist who uses fairy tales to shift the paradigm of society's expectations for women. Muriel Rukeyser wrote, "What would happen if one woman told the truth about her life? The world would split open." In this small volume poets bear witness to their truths. You will hear in their words the chutzpah to think that their poems can effect change in the world.

~ Ellen Goldberg
May, 2015

• *Act One* •

Fullerton

This poem is when my son is a baby, nursing a lot
and we're mostly past the hard part, he's eating
applesauce, mashed bananas, oatmeal, gummy bits
of grownup food along with all this milk, so I go out
don't remember why, tell his father *back soon*
or *couple hours* (or what I'm really thinking — no
not that) and go down to the Fullerton bus stop
wearing cut-off blue jeans, white sneakers and a red
t-shirt that says HEY CUBS, THIS IS THE YEAR!

I get whatever it is I've gone for and stand out
at another bus stop carrying packages, paper bags
I have to hold or set down to wait, there's no bus
all the time fills up with thinking (the baby and me
in a small van, driving out far to see the sky)
soon my breasts are aching, dripping, so I go back
to wherever I just came out of, the women's room
fold kleenex over my nipples inside their container
built like a suspension bridge, go back to the corner
step off the curb, look down the street, far down
where there's no bus, no bus, no bus, no sign of a bus
for my paper bags, aching breasts, damp kleenex
I put a thumb out, up at the necessary angle
and the Chrysler appears suddenly, silent, dark blue
or maybe it's even purple and the window slides
down like in a movie and he says *how far you going?*

We're on Lake Shore Drive in rush hour (if I had
that van, this'd still be a battle) sitting here deep in

creamy pale leather, my wet breasts throbbing
like he knows this, he nods toward my chest and says
are they real? he's driving past Oak Street Beach
left hand at ten o'clock, right hand in left breast
pocket slips a small folded case out of his jacket
eases it down between his legs where he opens it
takes out fifty-dollar bills, they are fifties, I look
twice, wondering who's on the fifty as he lays
them down, one at a time, on his thigh, sliding them
down the fabric, spreading the bills along his leg
in a narrow fan, hand steady as he drives the limit
barely moving his eyes, tipping his chin slightly
toward my breasts, his fingers still stroking
the fifties, his thigh, the open case between his legs —

At North Avenue his eyes turn right, to my nipples, rise
to my throat, eyes, fall down to my swollen wet breasts
he licks his lips and says again *how far you going?*
several minutes (hours, days, weeks) go by in three
or four or five seconds as I think about this man sucking
my baby's milk, about his fanned-out fifties, about escaping
from my marriage sooner than later, I think about those
things in less time than it takes you to read these words
before I say, Fullerton — I'm going up to Fullerton.

Define Me

Call me pretty.
Define me,
By the shape of my eyes,
By the color of my skin,
By the curve of my ass,
By the pout of my lips.

Call me smart.
Define me,
By my SAT scores,
By my GPA,
By my class load,
By my college admission.

Call me ugly.
Define me,
By the straightness of my teeth,
By the curl of my hair,
By the weight of my breasts,
By the size of my waist.

Call me a bitch.
Define me,
By the sharpness in my tone,
By my attitude,
By the strength of my leadership,
By my power.

Call me a woman.

Define me,
By my brain and my heart,
By my choices,
By my clothes,
By my reproductive system.

Or don't call me pretty,
Or smart,
Or ugly,
Or a bitch,
Or even a woman.
Define me as me.

Or don't define me at all.

Scarecrow's Daughter

What I need him to understand
is that I love the crows, the sheen
of them, the crowd of their voices,
the way their wings make that sound
like a field mouse running for its life
through dry grass, the blur of the fox.

At night on our twin posts, he feathers
his straw hand on my straw cheek,
plumps his shirt a little, stares down
between the rows of corn. Stars ignite
in the autumn darkness, I lean
in the wind toward the hem of the crop.

How I could rustle in my red-flowered
dress to the edge of the cornfield,
reach up my husks to the branches
bent down to meet me, pull myself
up. How I could see beyond
the farmhouse, the span of the road.

I've had enough of scaring things
away. Startling hungry eyes
from every stalk, when what I want to do
is tear back the green so that the sun smacks
full on the yellow meat of the cobs, offer
up ears for the feasting, whisper, *stay.*

I want everything to land on me, dig
into my straw-stuffed shoulders
and carry me up into the blue. They
would look beautiful, the crows, kernels
balanced in their beaks, whirling
close to my father, then peeling away.

The sunrise is lovely. October
is lovely. I can hear the harvesters
waking at the edges of dawn. How
I would climb down, husks crackling
as I landed. Weigh the unbearable
options. Settle on which way to run.

A Princess Doesn't Live Here

This girl's mother didn't raise a princess,
to sit around waiting to be kissed.
She knew not to bite into the poison apple
but grew her own instead.

The kings and queens in this child's house
resided in decks of cards where
the princes were all known as knaves,
names that warned of trouble ahead.

She learned how to build her house of bricks,
not straw or sticks to be blown away
by wolves clad in sheep skin who prey
on innocents or creep in on lonely nights.

This carpenter's daughter wore her own
seven league boots to take her round the world,
rubbing ancient lamps that kept their genies,
gathering riches that could not be bought ...

When she kissed the frogs, she knew
she kissed frogs, not treasures in disguise.
When she nibbled the cookie house
she was prepared to pay the price.

Before They Reheat the Rod

In the ancient city, they heated iron rods
and blinded all the daughters.

Then they told the daughters *Every man
is brave and beautiful.*

In that city, they blessed the girls' hands
and set them to spin in the dark.

Behind bronze gates, the daughters sang
the hymns almost as instructed,

but they sang in a language understood
only by birds of prey.

Listen. The wings of the blind daughters
summoned a wild sirocco wind

so that sand dunes buried the ancient city.
What endures now is the song.

Do you know it?
Whisper the words in your daughter's ear.

Requiem

~ for Nikki Elias

He kicked the door in.
let her name be blessed
There was a restraining order.
let her name be praised
There was a stalking order.
let her name be glorified
There was extra security at the school.
let her name be lifted up
Her two girls there watching.
let her name be graced in beauty
He shot her with an arrow and a gun.
let her name ascend in joy
She was buried under a freezing rain.
let her name ascend in joy
He shot her with an arrow and a gun.
let her name be graced in beauty
Her two girls there watching.
let her name be lifted up
There was extra security at the school.
let her name be glorified
There was a stalking order.
let her name be praised
There was a restraining order.
let her name be blessed
He kicked the door in.

So What

~ *For Areen Nashef and Yael Keinan,*
students at Jerusalem's Hand in Hand (Yad B'Yad) School,
one of the only bi-cultural, bilingual, integrated schools
for Arabs and Jews in Israel.

The idea right there in plain sight,
obvious as breathing with a hat on,
though few of their Israeli and
Palestinian neighbors and friends
and cousins could see it, their eyes
cataracted with fear. But for Areen
and Yael in first grade, it was easy.
Teachers filled the classroom with
Arabic and Hebrew, and so what
they had no words yet to talk to each other.
They used their hands, wrapped books
together, ate figs and pomegranates together,
played ball together under the olive trees.
So what if they disagreed and agreed
all the way up the ladder of grades,
they learned each other's languages
and listened, didn't they, heard with their
ears and toes and rows of desks, cluttered
and spattered with their complicated lives.
They spoke, didn't they, they understood,
their arms around each other's waists.
And their words rose with the years,
We don't blame each other for the
adults' mistakes, we are sisters.

The River Keeper

I gather the wood of a juniper
for her torso; river-washed twine
binds her cotton wood spine. Atop
her river clay mask a salt cedar sprig

headdress rustles and hums a desert
breeze. Her obsidian arrowhead eyes
reflect cumulus sky ciphers. A broken
wooden ruler for good measure. Strings

of rusty cans for arms and legs.
Earth Mother pictograms etch the wet sand.
The hymns of ancestral women
course through my grateful bones.

Beltane on the Land

naked women
make mud
like children
but on a grander scale
the pit is wide and deep
at the north end of the garden

they dig
with pitch forks and shovels
dig in hard soil
add cold, cold water
make mud
dark as chocolate
rough as sandpaper
thick worms head for shore
fat drops of warm rain
plop down from no clouds
pieces of sky for mud stew

some women
wear broad brimmed hats
sit on tidy blanket islands
in the meadow grass
they worry their skin might be torn by thorns

the fearless yell
and jump in
grab and slide
take one another down

and down again
full weight against full weight
against slippery skin

solid woman
one dark earth color
even her eyes
call to those still wearing pristine skin —

virgin
virgin
come in
come in
let this earth between your toes
between your legs
into your ears

slide down my strong back
over my head
my body will be your bridge
your bridge
into this good mud

taste it
rub your hands in your hair
lean against me
let my hands sand your skin

we are buried
in this wet earth
then held by sun and wind
until we are gray
skin taut and dry
cracked and open

• *Act Two* •

Martha, 1630

Branks: A device consisting of a metal frame for the head and a bit to restrain the tongue, formerly used to punish scolds.

1

It was nothing but the truth, what I said:
He *was* lazy. He smelled like a pig.
He hit me for no cause but that I spoke.

Anyway, 'twas for his own good –
I said what I said, hoping he'd go to work
or wash himself at the pump before he ate.

So what if I said it more than once?
He didn't hear the first time, nor the third
as far as I could tell. He never looked up.

So then I spoke louder, like you do
to one who is deaf or a little simple.
Yes, I cursed him – just once I cursed his name.

"Raise your voice, do you?" he said
so I turned my back and busied myself
at the stove, stirring the porridge oats.

I made it just the way he likes
but he was gone when I served it up
with a knob of butter I'd begged at the farm.

Before I could eat even a spoonful myself,
they came in, three of them, smiling, casual-like.
One of them held the thing. I knew what it was.

2

A boy once told me my cheek were pink like a fruit
but now 'tis raw where the bridle grips
and pus is crusted under the metal rods.

Was pride another sin? My hair once blonde
hasn't been washed: I've let it go to grease.
The headpiece rests on that join atop my skull

where bone meets bone. It must've been soft
when my newborn skull rested in mother's palm.
She warned me, my mam, told me to watch my tongue

and now my tongue's held down by the bit –
she was right, I always did speak my mind too much.
The sores on my lips make me think on that boy …

So many years since I learned to kiss.
So many years since I wanted to kiss.
Now when I make his porridge I hawk and spit.

The Ride

Inside this coach –
half pumpkin, half carriage –
the air is ripe.
I lean back against
one thick curved wall,
and its dampness seeps
into my borrowed dress
so that the ivory silk
clings like a second skin.
My heavy hair is slipping
from its snug pins – I feel it
curl around my face – while
over my head a moist seed
hangs by a yellow thread.
As the carriage bumps its way
over rocks and twigs, I watch the
seed swing this way and that,
like a pendulum gone wild. I open
my palm, and the seed drops into it.
Ahead, the ballroom waits,
lit with candles and a pulsing
that matches my own heartbeat –
no more breathy songs
smothered in soap bubbles,
no more pretend partners,
no more taking tentative shadow steps
within the confines of my kitchen –
when the carriage comes to a stop,

I don't wait for the coachman.
I push open the door
and step into my night.

Forgetting the Names

When life gets long, we begin
to forget the names,
names of those we've just met,
names of others who brushed by briefly,
profoundly long ago.

I'm forgetting one now,
the name of a young woman,
small like me, with dark curls,
two houses down in our
high desert, low-rent homes
on the Deschutes. Both of us
poor, both of us ripe with
first child, just weeks to bursting –
hers a son, mine a daughter.

I remember the fire,
that took her house one night
just days before I delivered.
The two of us stood in the crowd outside.
One blanket wrapped around us both.
Black silhouettes of phantom firemen
danced between the licks of flame.
I remember the smell of smoke,
the taste of loss.

Forgetting her name torments me today.
We held each other and wept.
Our swollen bellies pressed

as one in the orange glow. We wept
for our children soon to enter
this world of sudden surprise
with old soul eyes and
misplaced trust.

Does it matter? Forgetting her name?
The fire that night burned us together,
fused in timeless sisterhood.

A Freelancer's Interview With A Woman of Industry, 1982

She claimed her future chose her as a child. How triple garage doors
across from her home went up and down, up and down, breaking
the strict facade of that one-story yellow brick building.
Sleek black hearses entered, left at all hours,
with black windows and gray drapes.
Little else moved to draw her child's eye.

The dead came first. Then sprays of white carnations,
white football mums, roses, snapdragons and mourners.
Coffins left. Doors open and shut. The parking lot drained out
cars with headlights on, leaving
black puddles in the asphalt.

I stopped taking notes when she said she had invited childhood
friends
to bring over Barbie dolls. She played funeral director,
helping them wash, dress, and lay out Barbies and Kens
in shoe boxes. She made the girls pretend-tea to ease the choices
about casket liners. She growled whines of garage doors.

As an adult, she was pretty. Blonde. This young woman
in her expensive gray suit and white silk blouse.
She was proud of having climbed the rungs
of the management ladder
in a national funeral corporation
wearing low heeled pumps.
She thanked feminists for opportunities

for roles beyond washing and anointing bodies
and that Civil War trade of embalming
that women learned on battlefields.

I think of her sometimes.
My Barbies rode horseback.
A foreign exchange student from Kenya told me
his biggest surprise about America
was that not only did most people have a house,
the cars had houses too. How fast
the doors opened and shut.

The Coffin of Emmett Till

I cry every day. But I cry as I move.
~ Mamie Till-Mobley

It is the silence
the barn door slammed shut
on a child in the middle of the night
the way the river water
rushes, covers what it covers
the way the heavy lid
stays shut
stays shut
until she refuses
silence
the awful lid
her child shut
beneath the moon, the ink-black water
that covers
what they did – it took more
than one beating, it took the fan
of a cotton gin
it took a knot of barbed wire
it took
the fear of big white men
yet still
he floated up
and she refuses silence
and she names him
and she refuses
to bury this

boy beneath the lid
he's traveled far
all the way back
from any hole in Mississippi, far
from orders of that government
and it can't just be
a leaden box
of stones or bricks
it can't just be
a trick
with no boy there
on that returning train
a box big enough to fill
three graves
she refuses, she unseals
she needs to know
the way the distant river
and its little markets,
little houses,
sheriffs with their guns and beer and pop
the official state itself
Mississippi
would cover him
she would know
this is her child
from his well-made
slender
ankle bones
his sturdy legs
none of Emmett's body scarred
all the way up
up to his chin
she needs to
face him

face him

open it

Nineteen-Thirty-Eight

I remember the way my mother
answered when people asked
where she'd gone to school:

South Side High, 1938,
adding the year in the same breath
though I knew

she never graduated,
yanked out
when her father lost his job.

Now it was her turn
to make herself
useful, he told her.

Hadn't he put
food on the table
all her life and all her little sister's?

How necessary
to tell a lie like hers, to answer
South Side High, 1938, and smile

without betraying
the blaze in her chest, her envy
for the questioner who likely met

her own husband at some university.
But wasn't my mother *the lucky one,*
my grandfather was fond of telling her

even into my childhood, sometimes
in front of my friends, lucky
to have got my father, a college man

who sat beside her at a ballgame
in 1939? *Just look at her
who didn't finish high school!*

Didn't I tell her then it wouldn't matter?

Empty

She was a smart girl,
seventeen, youngest in her graduating class,
valedictorian on her way to Yale.
So smart in fact, she knew better
than to leave her mom's car
on empty.

She hated gas station restrooms,
(who could blame her?)
but after hours on the road,
too many Red Bulls,
she couldn't wait.
The grease monkey attendant
hands her a unisex key,
leering at her,
seems he has something
that couldn't wait either.

All she really remembers
is neon blue of flashing lights,
crimson red of a blood-soaked dress.
She doesn't remember crying,
but someone must have
heard her scream.

She sits in the waiting room,
hands wringing in her lap,
six weeks and she can still see
rope burns on her wrists,

and the scab where she started
to cut away her life,
but couldn't quite finish the job.

She doesn't drive anymore,
the thrill replaced now by terror.
She shields her eyes from the television
every time commercials for Chevron run.
The animated cars seem to taunt her;
memories returning now haunt her.

The army of protestors,
relentless chanting,
a woman throws
cooked beets at her feet.
Choose Life. Choose Life.
They rant.
They rage.

She asks her mother
if it's a mistake,
not *choosing life.*

Holding her daughter,
she quiets her trembling body,
lovingly whispers in her ear:

> *We are sweetheart;*
> *we're choosing yours.*

Breasts: A Poem in Two Parts

I.

About the same time my
oldest daughter confided

that her daddy's daddy
had nicknamed hers

when she was 12,
I looked online to see

if the euphemisms
had changed since I'd grown mine –

"Skeeter bites," it turns out,
is among an endless parade of

robust euphemisms no matter
what our eras:

Loblollies
Love Bubbles
Snuggle Pups
Blouse Bunnies
Rib Cushions
Double-Whammies
Hindenburgs
Pointer Sisters
Cupcakes

Flapjacks
Fun Bags
Flotation Devices
Chihuahuas
Spark Plugs
Spark Plugs?
Milk Shakes
Mam Glands
Mounds
Twin Peaks
Sweater Meat
McGuffeys
Knockers
Rack
Chesticles
Headlights
Hooters
Cha Chas
Casabas
The Gravitas Girls
The Upper balcony
Balloons
Bazongas
Gazongas
Bazooms
Bust bumps,
Melons
Jugs
Cans
And, of course,
Tits, Titties and Tatas

Or, as one Online dictionary claims
about breasts' origins, *seat of the emotions*,

and, like all seats, hands-off
for assessing and commenting,

especially by Grandpas and/or any
other boobs, the latter defined,

euphemistically, of course,
for example, as:

Nitwits
Dunces
Fatheads
Fools
Goofs
Goons
Imbeciles
Jerks.

      II.

Breasts in a young granddaughter
just now starting to *girl up* her mother reports.

I don't mention that on our side of the family, *the girls*
start to *grandma down* in our twenties –

genetics predisposed to early-onset gravity.
Instead, I remember three best friends from fifth grade

who met at the corner grocery store after school
to eat up the candy of adolescence.

Taken over by our bodies' and our parents' commands,
the three of us formed a kind of paramilitary unit.

We stood in line, comparing equipment
and then made up rules and names.

Leslie, for obvious reasons,
called hers Flopsy and Mopsy.

Irene, with a perfectly matched set,
settled on Salt and Pepper.

Two cup sizes younger and just starting to sprout,
I picked Rosebud and Petunia Bud.

Whenever any one of the three of us
announced, *Roll Call* –

no matter where we stood –
classroom, berry patch,

crossing the street, in the aisles of Boots Grocery –
we *had* to hoist our gear and present loud and clear.

Not that subterfuge wasn't allowed.
We could cross our arms or not.

Lift with the open palm
or the back of the hand,

but no fair whispering so someone standing
six feet away couldn't hear.   .

And like all roll calls, we had to take turns,
no announcing all at once.

FLOPSY
MOPSY

SALT
PEPPER

PETUNIA BUD
ROSEBUD

1955, 1956, 1957, we played our game,
with 1958 ending the parade.

By ninth grade, it was clear there were
just two classes of girls:

The As to Bs and the Cs to Ds.
Among the latter, we could see we were facing

a lifetime of confinement in that
old French prison, the brassière.

Acknowledgments

We gratefully acknowledge the following publications in which these poems first appeared:

"Fullerton" by Judith Arcana was first published in *5AM*, Summer 2011

"Before They Reheat the Rod" by Penelope Scambly Schott first appeared in her book, *How I Became an Historian*

"So What" by Fran Payne Adler was previously published (with photo of Areen and Yael, and video interview) by *Hand in Hand Center for Jewish-Arab Education in Israel*

"The River Keeper" by Marilyn Stablein was first published as part of a trilogy of poems in "A Feminist Anthology - Part II" edited by Dale Harris, *Malpais Review*, Vol.5 No. 2, Autumn 2014)

"Beltane on the Land" by Ila Suzanne Gray previously appeared in We'Moon '97 (Mother Tongue Ink)

"Martha, 1630" by Judith Barrington was first published in *Southward Journal* and appears in *The Conversation* (Salmon Poetry, 2015)

"The Ride" by Linda Ferguson was previously published in the Summer 2013 issue of *VoiceCatcher: Journal of Women's Voices & Visions*

"Nineteen-Thirty-Eight" by Andrea Hollander was first published in *Prairie Schooner 77:3* (Fall 2003); subsequently it was included in the following individual collections by Andrea Hollander: *Woman in the Painting* (Autumn House Press, 2006) and *Landscape with Female Figure: New & Selected Poems, 1982 – 2012* (Autumn House Press, 2013)

"Empty" by Shawn Aveningo was first published in *The Oddity*, a publication of UC Davis

Contributors

Ellen Goldberg, Editor, is the winner of the 2011 Robin Becker Chapbook award for *Each Perfect One* (Seven Kitchens Press). Her first book of poems was *Meeting Street*, and she's been published in *Naming: An Anthology of Eight Women*, *Calyx*, *Windfall*, *Columbia Sun*, *Silo* and *Lyric Garden*. She's had grants to perform and teach writing in Portland schools and the community. She's performed in and organized many poetry events including *The Wayback* and most recently, *Of Course I'm a Feminist!* She's a member of the 29th Street Writers.

• Act One •

Judith Arcana's poems, stories and essays are in journals and anthologies, online and on paper. Her poetry collections are *What If Your Mother*, *4th Period English*, *The Parachute Jump Effect* and *The Water Portfolio*, a set of three lyric broadsides. Judith's story, *Soon To Be A Major Motion Picture* (fiction), won the first Minerva Rising Prose Prize – published as a chapbook in 2015. <juditharcana.com>

Elise Kuechle is a sophomore at Oregon Episcopal School. In her free time, she enjoys writing poetry and reading. Elise is on her school's debate team where she competes in policy debate and expository speaking. For the past two years, she has been a member of OES's state champion OBOB (Oregon Battle of the Books) team. Elise enjoys acting and most recently portrayed Conrade in *Much Ado About Nothing*. In the future, she hopes to continue writing lots of poetry!

Brittney Corrigan is the author of the poetry collection *Navigation* (The Habit of Rainy Nights Press, 2012) and the chapbook *40 Weeks* (Finishing Line Press, 2012). Her poems have appeared widely in journals and anthologies, and she is the poetry editor for the online journal *Hyperlexia: poetry and prose about the autism spectrum* (hyperlexiajournal.com). Brittney lives in Portland, Oregon, where she is both an alumna and employee of Reed College. <brittneycorrigan.com>

Carlyn Syvanen retired from Portland Public Schools to move to Sequim, Washington where she and her husband keep themselves busy with orchard, garden and chickens. She manages to travel to far places as often as possible and to write poetry when the beauty or the pain of this world moves her.

Penelope Scambly Schott's verse biography of Puritan dissident Anne Hutchinson, *A Is for Anne: Mistress Hutchinson Disturbs the Commonwealth*, received an Oregon Book Award. Other books about women in history include *Penelope: The Story of the Half-Scalped Woman* and *Lily Was a Goddess, Lily Was a Whore*. "Before They Reheat the Rod" appeared in her newest book, *How I Became an Historian*. She lives in Portland and Dufur, Oregon where she teaches an annual poetry workshop.

Pam Crow's poetry collection, *Inside this House,* was published by Main Street Rag press in 2007. Her poems have appeared in numerous literary journals, including *Ploughshares, Southern Poetry Review* and *Calyx,* and anthologized in *The Bedford Introduction to Literature.* She was a recipient of the Astraea Emerging Lesbian Writer's award. Pam lives in Portland, Oregon where she works as a clinical social worker.

Frances Payne Adler is the author of *Making of a Matriot* (Red Hen Press); *Raising The Tents* (Calyx Books); *When The Bough Breaks: Pregnancy and the Legacy of Addiction* (NewSage Press), and others. Adler also co-edited *Fire and Ink: An Anthology of Social Action Writing* (University of Arizona Press). Her current collaborative work is *Dare I Call You Cousin*, about the Israeli-Palestinian conflict. Adler, Professor Emerita and founder of the Creative Writing & Social Action Program at California State University Monterey Bay, lives in Portland, Oregon.

Marilyn Stablein is the author of twelve books including *Splitting Hard Ground*, winner of the New Mexico Book Award and the National Federation of Press Women's Book Award. Other books include a Himalayan memoir, *Sleeping in Caves* and a collection of eco-essays, *Climate of Extremes: Landscape and Imagination*. A former book critic for *The Seattle Times*, she teaches memoir and an introduction to artist books in the Mountain Writers Series and exhibits her collage and artist books internationally. <marilynstablein.com>

Ila Suzanne Gray is a passionate feminist working on her fourth collection of poetry. Her poem *Then There Were the Wimmin* was produced as performance art at the Los Angeles Women's Building. She collaborated with Kay Gardner on the oratorio *Ouroboros: Seasons of Life, A Woman's Passage*. Her poems appear in We'Moon Calendars and other pagan, lesbian and literary journals including *Gertrude* and *Windfall: A Journal of Poetry of Place*.

• Act Two •

Judith Barrington is the author of four volumes of poetry, most recently, *The Conversation*, published by Salmon poets. The title poem won the Gregory O'Donoghue International Poetry Prize, and the judge, Thomas McCarthy wrote; "this is a brilliant technical achievement; it reminds us all that great poetry is both fine thinking and achieved style..." Her *Lifesaving: A Memoir* won the Lambda Book Award and her *Writing the Memoir: From Truth to Art* is a bestseller.

Linda Ferguson's poetry, fiction and essays have been published in numerous journals, including *VoiceCatcher Journal, The Santa Fe Literary Review, The Milo Review* and *Saranac Review*. She's won awards from the Oregon Poetry Association, received the Perceptions 2013 award for nonfiction and was nominated for a Pushcart Prize for fiction. She's also the author of a poetry chapbook, *Baila Conmigo*, and teaches creative writing for adults and children. <www.bylindaferguson. blogspot.com>

Gail Barker left her native New York arms flailing with youth, spent time in San Francisco, British Columbia, Bend, Eugene, and landed in Portland thirty years ago. Today she lives in Milwaukie and serves on the Milwaukie Poetry Series Committee. Her poems have been published in *Faultline*, *VoiceCatcher*, and *The William Stafford Newsletter*. She drinks from the deep well of poetry and sometimes adds her own.

Tricia Knoll is a Portland poet – with an intense interest in both feminism and eco-poetry. Her chapbook *Urban Wild* came out in 2014 from Finishing Line Press and focuses on the interactions of humans and wildlife in urban (mostly Oregon) habitat. Her poems have appeared in many journals including *CALYX Journal*, *Windfall*, *Catch & Release – The Literary Blog of Columbia Journal*, *Written River – A Journal of Eco-Poetics* and many others. Two of her poems have been nominated for Pushcart Prizes. <triciaknoll.com>

A founding member of Airlie Press, **Carter McKenzie** is the author of the chapbook *Naming Departure* and a full-length book of poetry *Out of Refusal*. Her work has appeared in various journals and anthologies, including *What the River Brings: Oregon River Poems*, *Canary*, and *The Berkeley Poets Cooperative: A History of the Times*. She offers poetry sessions for adults as well as children in Eugene and surrounding rural areas. She lives in the Cascade Foothills with her youngest daughter.

Andrea Hollander's fourth poetry collection, *Landscape with Female Figure*, was a finalist for the 2014 Oregon Book Award. Other honors include the Nicholas Roerich Poetry Prize, a Pushcart Prize for memoir, an Oregon Literary Fellowship, and two fellowships from the National Endowment for the Arts. Hollander moved to Portland in 2011, after 22 years as the Writer-in-Residence at Lyon College, where she won the Williamson Prize for Teaching Excellence. She now conducts workshops at the Attic Institute and Mountain Writers.

Shawn Aveningo is a globally published poet whose work has appeared in over 80 literary journals and anthologies, including LA's *poeticdiversity* who recently nominated her poetry for a Pushcart. She is co-founder of The Poetry Box® and web-designer for *VoiceCatcher: a journal of women's voices & visions*. Shawn's a proud mother of three who believes poetry is the perfect literary art form for today's fast-paced world, due to its power to stir emotion in less than two minutes. <redshoepoet.com>

In 2003, at age 58, **Sharon Wood Wortman** crossed the bridge of journalism to explore spoken word poetry and memoir. In 2009, she performed her one-woman show, *The Bridge Lady*, at Portland's Shoebox Theatre, and, in February 2011, a 17-minute monologue, same title, for *The Moth Radio Hour*, before a live audience of 2,500, at the Arlene Schnitzer Concert Hall. With four children, 11 grandchildren 1 great-grand, an 18-year-old dog, and a good husband competing for her focus, Sharon attends faithfully to her membership in the 29th Street Writers.

About Soapstone

Soapstone is a 501(c)(3) nonprofit organization, whose mission is to bring people together to celebrate and support the work of women writers.

Soapstone, a grassroots organization since 1992, was originally formed to provide writing residencies for women at a retreat in Oregon's Coast Range. The energy for the project grew out of the women's movement of the 1970s and 80s. Their focus was on women writers, who face special obstacles in finding the time and space for serious writing. They liked the notion that a group of ordinary people could work together to make something important happen in their community, without a founding bequest or permanent benefactor, a fancy office, high salaries, or exclusive fundraising events.

Soapstone has provided residencies to over 375 writers from 1998 through 2010. They are proud of what they have made possible over these past two decades and grateful to everyone who has participated in any way. The Soapstone property was sold in November of 2013 after placing a conservation easement on the property through the North Coast Land Conservancy, ensuring that it will be protected into perpetuity. Their passionate commitment to supporting women writers has not in any way faded. Nor has their commitment to fostering community. With the proceeds from the sale of the property along with a modest endowment they will continue to make a unique contribution to Oregon and Southwest Washington's literary community by offering small grants for ad hoc events, such as the "Of Course, I'm a Feminist!" reading and study groups celebrating women writers.

For More Information, please visit www.soapstone.org.

About The Poetry Box

The Poetry Box® was founded in 2011 by Shawn Aveningo & Robert R. Sanders, who whole-heartedly believe that every day spent with the people you love, doing what you love, is a moment in life worth celebrating.

It all started out as our way to help people memorialize the special milestones in their lives by melding custom poems with photographic artwork for anniversaries, birthdays, holidays and other special occasions. Robert and Shawn then expanded on their shared passion for creating poetry and art with the introduction of The Poetry Box® Book Publishing.

Robert and Shawn continue to celebrate the talents of their fellow artisans and writers. In addition to publishing two themed journals per year (*The Poeming Pigeon – A Literary Journal of Poetry*), The Poetry Box® now offers professional book design and publishing.

And as always, The Poetry Box® believes in giving back to the community. Each month a portion of all sales benefit a different charity. For a complete list of the charities currently supported, please visit the Giving Back page on their website at www.ThePoetryBox.com.

Feel free to visit The Poetry Box® online bookstore, where you'll find more books including:

Keeping It Weird: Poems & Stories of Portland, Oregon

Verse on the Vine: A Celebration of Community, Poetry, Art & Wine

The Way a Woman Knows by Carolyn Martin

Poeming Pigeons: Poems about Birds

———— *Order Form* ————

Need more copies for friends and family? No problem. We've got you covered with two convenient ways to order:

1. Go to our website at www.thePoetryBox.com and click on Bookstore.

or

2. Fill out the order form. Email it to Shawn@thePoetryBox.com or mail it to: The Poetry Box, 2228 NW 159th Pl, Beaverton, OR 97006.

Name: _____

Shipping Address: _____

_____

Phone Number: (____) _____

Email Address: _____@_____

Payment Method: __Cash __Check __PayPal Invoice __Credit Card

Credit Card #: _____ CCV _____

Expiration Date: _____ Signature: _____

Of Course I'm a Feminist! # of Copies: _____

x $10.00: _____

Plus Shipping & Handling: _____
($3 per book, or $7.95 for 3 or more books)

Order Total: _____

Thank You!

Made in the USA
San Bernardino, CA
14 November 2018